Guidelines for

Teaching Contracts

SETTING UP PAYMENT RULES FROM THE OUTSET

Janine Bray-Mueller

BoD – Books on Demand, Norderstedt,
Germany

Bibliografische Information der Deutschen
Nationalbibliotek:
Die Deutsche Nationalbibliothek verzeichnet diese
Publikation in der Deutschen Nationalbibliografie;
detaillierte bibliografische Daten sind im Internet über
http://dnb.dnb.de abrufbar.

Deutsche Nationalbibliotek bibliographic information:
The German National Library lists this publication in the
Deutsche Nationalbibliografie; Detailed bibliographic data
are available on the Internet at http://dnb.dnb.de.

Printed and published by
BoD-Books on Demand, Norderstedt,

ISBN 978-3-7543 4593-1

Janine Bray-Mueller
Le Haut Quérant
56120 Pleugriffet, France
www.braymueller.com

Guidelines for Teaching Contracts is a republished, completely revised short book version and is reprinted with permission from *The Teacher's Guide to Pricing Matters*, by Janine Bray-Mueller, 2019, BoD - Books on Demand, Norderstedt, Germany

Book Layout © 2013 BookDesignTemplates.com
Chapter dividing line from pngtree.com (commercial free)
Book Cover Images by Clker-Free-Vector-Images / 29565 and OpenClipart-Vectors / 27398 from Pixabay
(Pixabay Licence: Free for commercial use/No attribution required)

Manufactured and published by BoD - Books on Demand, Norderstedt, Germany
Guidelines for Teaching Contracts / Janine Bray-Mueller
1st Edition
ISBN 978-3-7543 4593-1

QUICK READS FOR BUSY FREELANCERS

Contents

Guidelines for

Teaching Contracts

SETTING UP PAYMENT RULES FROM THE OUTSET

NOTE: **Guidelines for Teaching Contracts** *is a republished, completely revised short book version of chapters previously published under The Teacher's Guide to Pricing Matters, by Janine Bray-Mueller, 2019, BoD - Books on Demand, Norderstedt, Germany.*

Janine Bray-Mueller

Do You Need Teaching Contracts?

There are no rules (governing a teaching service) unless you put them into place yourself

That is why you should always set payment rules from the beginning

As a foundation for your work, contracts set up shared communications between yourself and the customer concerning receiving and giving tuition.

It also sets the groundwork for negotiations when things go wrong.

How to avoid late paying students

What happens when students don't pay or forget to pay on time? Well... There are no rules unless you put them there yourself.

The same is true for freelance teachers if they don't want to suffer high blood pressure because they haven't (yet) been paid. When a teacher's income is jeopardised, the iron ball of desperation rolls. Its metal sound is the first grinding note that 'tolls death' for any entrepreneurial freelance teaching service.

- Should I ignore the receivable (the debt)? Or extend the time and allow the student to pay later (*and* continue working with them)?

- Should I forget the receivable? Can I accept losing not just my money but also my time as well?

- Should I sue? (Can I afford to go to court?)

- Should I 'fire' the student and lose future business with them?

- Should I give incentive discounts to pay early and to pay on time?

- And so on...

Make rules (pay upfront *and* have a contract)

How do you make sure you are paid on time? The easiest method is to make rules in your business and stick to them. It's far better to lose a non-paying student than to have sleepless nights when you cannot pay your bills.

When you have your student sitting before you, make sure you define:

1. The scope of lessons, course, seminar-workshop and time frame

2. The rules for cancelling lessons or seminar-workshops

3. When the student is expected to pay and what happens when payment is late (direct and associate customers)

Who are direct customers?

Your direct customers are private students and companies you have *found and won yourself* through your marketing efforts.

Who are associate customers?

Associate customers (schools and institutes), on the other hand, find students and customer *for you*. You have not been involved in finding these students yourself.

Penalty clauses for late or breach of payments

Penalty clauses are not uncommon in commercial businesses, especially when the ordered services and delivery times are critical.

Should *penalty clauses* be included when customers don't pay on time or cancel too late? The colleagues most at risk provide large training projects (such as workshops and speaker presentations). They have to weigh the consequences of not being paid (without penalty) against 'prestige' factors.

- Does the contracted work present (a much-desired) future opportunity in their careers? For example, TED Talks.

- Would the size and reputation of the company on the commercial, industrial, or educational markets be an important asset to their portfolios?

A penalty is not normally necessary for private students unless we heed **Marcus Tullius Cicero (106–43 B.C.) statement** still used today: *'the exception that proves the rule.'*[1]

Let's face it. Some individuals can become the worst repeat culprits. For these clients, late cancellation penalties (loss of

---

[1] Marcus Tullius Cicero (106–43 B.C.) statement *'exceptio probat regulam in casibus non exceptis'* was given in a speech during the defence of Lucius Cornellius Balbus. Its literal translation is: *the exception proves the rule in cases not excepted.*

lesson plus the lesson fee) must apply for all our students and not just companies. Be aware that company managers may not care about the penalty clause because it's not their money. However, private customers feel (personal) financial pain. So they become much more aware of the consequences when they don't show up, cancel too late, or pay too late.

Penalty clauses in the European Union (EU)

It is good to know that the European Union has created support programmes targeting small and medium-sized enterprises (SMEs). Teaching freelance services are also considered SMEs and fall under the protective *'Directive 2011/7/EU of the European Parliament and of the Council of 16 February 2011 on combating late payment in commercial transactions Text with EEA relevance.'* You can obtain more information by visiting the following EU web pages:

- The **2011/7/EU Directive** (available in several languages): https://bit.ly/EU_Directive_2011

- The **EU Late Payment Directive** can be found on:

  https://bit.ly/EU_LatePaymentDirective

- **Statutory interest rates** (%/year**) for late payments in all EU countries** can be found on:

  https://bit.ly/EU_LatePayments_PerCent

Finally, it's your decision in the end when clients do **not** respect your *agreed-to-and-signed* rules laid out in your contract.

Ask for upfront payments

Service providers:

- What happens when you want to park your car at the airport? You either pay beforehand as you enter the car park or before you leave the premises.

- Do you believe fortune-tellers will accept payment for their services only after you leave their tent at a fairground? Likewise, when you telephone a clairvoyant to read the stars and predict your future, your telephone service provider deducts their fee automatically.

- At the time of writing this book, most software and web services insist on *subscription* fees.

Product suppliers:

- What happens when you go into an art shop supplying paper, brushes, or watercolours? You have to pay before you can take the items with you.

- Can you help yourself to a supermarket item on credit? No, you cannot.

- Can you avoid paying beforehand when you purchase something on the Internet? Again, no.

Cultivate the same attitude. Ask customers to pay upfront.

—Expect your fees to be paid in advance—

When upfront payments are not possible

Educational institutions are renown late payers. French universities, for example, have an infamous reputation for paying late. I've been told that six months is the shortest period before French colleagues are paid.

Is there any hope of changing their attitude to this situation? Probably not.

Educational institutions adhere to internal payment policies that make it impossible to pay freelancers in advance—controls that prevent fast payments when invoices are received.

First, enquire about their payment policies. Then, decide whether you can accept them based on your personal financial requirements. Can you plan your financial outlays around their late payments? Or is it better to decide *against* working for them?

Whatever your decision, ensure your students (or company representatives) accept *your* rules and regulations—as in signing *your* teaching service contract.

Set the rules at the first meeting

Large companies or educational institutions will respect an agreement signed by the responsible person(s). When customers sign and accept your contract rules, you too have to countersign and agree to the regulations stipulated in them.

Your contract is binding for *both* of you.

If you keep to the rules, your customers will keep to them as well. But when they don't pay, you keep to your side of the contract and cancel lessons until payment arrives or paid according to the terms stipulated within your contract.

A contract is a form of reality check

Contracts and advance payments are a simple reality check. When both sides respect the contract, you can work together. However, if one side doesn't respect the agreement, hassle and stress can be expected.

It's not about being inflexible. On the contrary, there is always room for flexibility. But take heed because potential problems can lurk behind innocent-looking direction changes:

- The question of *respect* is one such issue.

  How far does the role of respect infiltrate your communication with the student? For example, can you still be motivated when your student does not respect your time? You have other commitments in your life.

- The question of whether to **withhold *(or cancel)* your lesson or the seminar-workshop** is another.

  Again, your decision *may* depend on whether your customers can influence future customers and word-of-mouth referrals.

- The question of **discounts** is another slippery slope that only you, the freelance teacher, can decide.

  Do you want to offer an incentive discount for paying promptly? Do you want a penalty clause that charges a late payment interest?

  I believe discounts devalue your service. But, again, it remains *your* decision.

These are *all* slippery slopes.

Everything sounds gloomier than it really is. After all, Murphy's Law states, *'Anything that can go wrong will go wrong.'* What I can say, however, is that a teaching service contract helps you circumvent many possible Murphy problems from escalating into serious issues.

Remember—a contract is a reality check plan for the freelance teacher because:

- When a freelance teacher's income is jeopardised, and bills cannot be paid, they go out of business.

- Contract rules must be agreed upon at the meeting when a private student (business or company customer) enrols in your course.

- Freelance teachers *can* lose students when they impose the consequences of non-adherence to rules written in the contract.

Are Teaching Contracts Useful?

Once upon a time, there lived a Chinese emperor who dearly wanted a beautiful black-lacquered box painted with a graceful picture of a heron—a symbol of strength, purity, patience, and long life. Finally, a local artist was found. He informed the emperor he could collect his box at the end of the month.

In great anticipation, the emperor arrived, but the box wasn't ready. Full of apologies, the artist asked him to come back the following month—then at the end of the year, then the following year, and then the next year, and so on, until ten years had passed. Finally, the emperor lost patience and insisted on the return of his lacquered box. At that point, the artist painted the most beautiful heron on the lid of the box the emperor had ever seen in a couple of brush strokes.

The anger evaporated to be replaced by awe and wonder. The emperor asked the artist his price for the exquisite work of art. The artist requested 10,000 yuan—a fortune. The emperor was visibly shocked. Outraged, he demanded with what right he could claim such a high price for less than two minutes' brushwork.

Bowing low, the artist took the emperor into the back room of his home. Thousands of silk panels were hanging from the ceiling—each panel filled with dozens of painted herons depicting every imaginable situation during its life.

'The price,' the artist replied, 'is not for two minutes' brushwork but for a lifetime learning how to paint the heron exactly as you imagined.'

This well-known story illustrates how misunderstandings and conflicts arise when the opportunity presents itself. Notably, when nothing has been recorded in writing. A contract goes a long way to ensure such misunderstandings are avoided.

Supplier *versus* Service Provider

In many countries, commercial payment laws distinguish between service providers and suppliers of commodities. Most of our customers, however, mentally classify tuition as a *product* supplied by a freelance teacher. They do not think 'teaching' is a *service,* but believe teaching freelancers are *suppliers—*an incorrect label.

For example, *suppliers* sell printer paper or toner and frequently apply set payment deadlines of 30, 60 or 90 days. A teaching business, on the other hand, is a *service provider* and sells time and knowledge. Consequently, service providers follow different payment terms.

The least complicated method to avoid *service* versus *supplier* issues is a well-prepared *service-provider* contract.

And by the way, it also projects a professional image, creates a certain amount of protection, and possibly changes your own perception towards your teaching business.

Are teaching service contracts necessary?

The straightforward answer is *yes*. You require a teaching service contract with *all* your customers. A contract safeguards your own peace of mind when payment problems loom and the seas turn rough. Consider it as your protection— a plan against difficulties with your customers at some future date.

However, teaching service contracts *also* protect your clients when an untoward mishap hinders *you* from giving your tuition.

Contract priorities

Priority must be given in laying out firm payment policies for your business. It is your only legal and binding proof of an agreement between you and your customers.

Remember, 80 per cent of businesses fail because they run out of money. A regular income—a steady cash flow—keeps your teaching business alive. Freelancers may have to resort to costly bank overdrafts if payments slow down (or not even be paid). Contracts help to control and avoid such issues.

It also secures a legally sound footing when making claims for monies due. Without being unduly morbid, it's the only proof your inheritors (or lawyer) will have to claim monies due to you should the occasion arise.

In fact, what is the first question asked when things turn sour?

Do you have a contract?

A lawyer's job (and your life) will be a lot easier and keep costs down when you have one.

What Goes Into a Contract?

A lawyer will guarantee your contract is written correctly. But they are most likely not yet affordable for beginning freelancers. So, in this case, a self-made contract must suffice. However, even self-made contracts follow a few rules.

Basic requirements

A contract is not valid unless it has *a date, signatures,* and the *names and addresses* of the parties involved. Practical is also additional information, such as e-mail addresses and telephone numbers. The following details have to be included in a contract:

Business customers:

1. Your contact information and that of the responsible person signing the contract

2. Students' names and contact details

3. Location of lessons and working conditions

4. Number of classes and frequency (or seminar-workshops)

5. Start and finish dates

6. Expiry date (for completing unused contracted lessons or seminar-workshops)

7. Prices and payment conditions

8. Materials and equipment required and/or provided

9. Travel costs, mileage, and whether the travelling time is included

10. IT availability (computer and internet technology)

11. Expected customer performance, objectives and/or aims

Private students:

1. Contact details including postal address

2. Where the lessons take place

3. Number of lessons and frequency

4. Start and finish dates

5. Expiry date (for using up unused contracted lessons)

6. Prices and payment conditions

7. Materials and equipment required or to be provided

8. Travel costs, mileage and whether the travelling time is included

9. Expected performance, objectives and/or aims

Further considerations

- Are direct and associate customers' prices different?

- Preparation time: curriculum planning, lessons, classes, seminar-workshops

- Are several contracts needed to meet different student requirements and/or for differently focused courses?

- Can copyright issues develop between you and your business customers and educational institutions?

- Travel time. Are breaks included when classes are back-to-back (i.e., consecutive) within large companies?

What Usually Gets Forgotten?

Freelance language teachers need to include clauses that are far too often overlooked until an (unfortunate) event happens. The following are three typically forgotten examples:

1. Cancellation policies

- *Regulate **absenteeism** when students become conspicuous by their absence.*

We've all suffered from cancellations or 'no-shows' in our careers. But, when it gets out of control, it's frustrating as well. Yes, absenteeism severely reduces, limits, and can even wipe out your annual income target. But it also has other follow-up issues, such as loss of motivation.

My freelancing career has shown that business customers with their (un)planned business meetings and trips are the worst culprits. They are cancelled at short notice (if at all), and they expect cancelled classes to be postponed with nary a thought about the freelancer's lost revenue.

Other examples I've run into are:

- *'I'm stuck in the middle of a major traffic jam.'*

- The student is suddenly sick

- The student, family member, friend, or colleague has had an accident, a problem, or whatever

- It's a beautiful and sunny day. They've been invited to a barbecue and have 'forgotten' your lesson appointment

And so on...

Have you thought about short-notice cancellations that block a much sought-after time slot but is never long enough for a new student? In my freelancing career, these were the early morning and evening time slots. Here is one such case I've had to deal with in my career:

'I can't come for the next seven weeks. I have an internal company course, followed by several business trips [which are not possible to move to another day of the week]*, and then I'm on holiday...'*

TIP: If new students don't turn up and do not reply to your e-mails, try to telephone them. It's a chance to discover why the student is no longer coming—and gives an opportunity to win back the student.

My teaching contract requires a 48-hour minimum notice; otherwise, the lesson must be paid. However, when several weeks' absence from planned lessons is expected (such as holidays or longer business trips), two weeks' notice is the minimum notice requirement.

2. Sickness

- *Insert a clause dealing with **sickness**, and for other '**forces beyond our control**' when either the teacher or the student becomes sick.*

Yes, these things *do* happen.

3. Late payment policies

- *Have you planned for **forgotten payments** or **non-payments**? What about **recurring late payments**?*

Have you prepared a clause in your service contract that covers potential payments problems? For example, you can bring out the contract to remind the defaulting customer if payments are delayed. But, of course, the cleanest and most effective solution is to require direct customers to **pay in advance**.

Being paid in advance is so important for a freelance teacher's survival, I am going to repeat it:

HAVE CUSTOMERS PAY **IN ADVANCE**

A PAYMENT-IN-ADVANCE policy has at least two benefits:

1. Because students have already paid, it's a great incentive to show up for lessons.

2. It's normal to feel exasperated when your timetable becomes lesson-bare because students fail to turn up or cancel classes at too short notice (forfeiting their payment). But your *time* is not lost. In fact, you have gained *extra* time. Since your defaulting student has already paid in advance, you now have the luxury of investing your newly won time to further your teaching business.

What activities could you undertake to further your teaching business?

- Student acquisition tasks, marketing tasks, or preparing leverage products such as supplying learning resources (e.g., audio and video files/downloads, books, and worksheets).

The bare truth in making a stand at the very first lesson

This means, of course, you have to take a stand. Make no mistake—this takes courage. When you haven't been paid, cancel lessons or classes **immediately**.

- The student has arrived and is standing on your doorstep. Unfortunately, you haven't yet received your fee. Without payment—cancel the lesson.

- Your expected payment hasn't been paid into your bank account—telephone the company representative to cancel classes until you have received your expected fee.

You *will* feel terrible, but remind yourself that if you let the lack of payment slip once—it will happen again and again. And inevitably, it will be the same student who consistently pays late.

What is going to happen when you cancel the lesson(s)?

1. First, you'll feel embarrassed. And you will believe you're going to lose the student or company. Take a deep breath and allow logic to take control over your panic. Common sense will tell you how you've saved yourself a lot of future problems when customers don't pay or never pay on time.

2. Try to overcome your embarrassment as you inform them: *Sorry, I didn't reserve a time slot for the lesson as you haven't paid yet. I was going to contact you later to see what had happened—to ask whether you had forgotten?*

3. I've noticed that students feel equally embarrassed about their forgetfulness. But, in general, they then pay quickly, and you are relieved. Because, when they don't pay, then you have saved yourself from a problematical student.

You have reasserted your authority as a teaching service provider and business person. You have cleared the atmosphere from future *misunderstandings* or *forgetfulness*. In particular about expecting them to pay your fees promptly.

As a professional, you expect your customers to respect your time preparing and carrying out the agreed-upon tuition.

And if the student continues to pay late?

Again, refer to the contract terms they have agreed upon and be prepared to lose the customer. You do not need customers who are unwilling to pay you timely for your teaching service.

When Should You Ask a Lawyer?

It is highly recommended to have any service contract checked by a lawyer to pick up possible loopholes in the agreement or rewrite unworkable language in the eyes of the law.

—We are trained teachers, not qualified lawyers—

Ask a lawyer for help, when:

- Contracts are complicated, beyond the usual scope of teaching activities, or

- They involve potential risks, such as the use of sensitive company information

When customers want changes to the contract

What is the recommended procedure when the customer questions the one or other clause in your contract? What if the customer wants to rewrite (or remove) one or more of your contract clauses? Or want to change the wording? What do you need to consider?

A recommended procedure:

1. If a business or associate customer is involved in asking for changes, make sure you talk with the representative with whom you negotiated your teaching service.

2. Based on your discussions, be open and offer alternative wording if requested 'within reason.' However, ask for time to ask a lawyer should you feel the business or associate customer's demands are 'out of the ordinary.' For example, please seek a lawyer for assistance when:

   a. They have (problematical) provisions they want to be added, which go beyond your teaching service parameters, or

   b. They want changes to payment terms or reimbursements amounts beyond 'the norm,' or

   c. They want changes to proprietary rights (copyrights) of materials you've produced yourself to prepare for or during the tuition or seminar-workshop.

3. The course or seminar-workshop content or time frame changes that deviate from those set out in the contract are signals to change the agreement yourself (the teaching scope offer and/or the prices).

Check List

What details must be included in a Teaching Service Contract?

**Teaching Service Contracts
(Behavioural and Cultural issues)**

Excepting for restrictions on gender-related issues in countries that forbid men and women to share the same classroom, I've not heard of other cultural problems influencing teaching and teaching service contracts. I would be interested to hear of any cultural issues that may influence a freelance teacher's work contract or prompt payment.

Add the details particular to your teaching niche

1.	GENERAL: Business customers
1.1	Contact information of the responsible person
1.2	The names of all attending students and their contact information **NOTE**: *A delay may occur when the company is still placing people into groups.*
1.3	The location, and which office or room? Time of classes? Are classes back-to-back, i.e., consecutive? Coffee and lunch breaks included?
1.4	Equipment and materials required and/or provided
1.5	How many lessons (seminar-workshops) have been booked? How often do classes take place in a week/month?
1.6	The start and finish dates
1.7	The expiry date for all remaining and unused classes

1.8	Payment conditions (e.g., hourly rates, per week, per course, or seminar-workshop)
1.9	Travel costs (e.g., bus, train, parking) and car kilometre or mileage allowance. Is travelling time included?
1.10	Cancellation policies for when students (or the teacher) are absent (e.g., sickness, holidays)

2.	GENERAL: Private students and Minors (see also ONLINE MINOR STUDENTS on page 62)
2.1	Contact information, including postal address
2.2	The place and times of lessons
2.3	How often do the lessons take place? How many have been agreed and booked?
2.4	The start and finish dates
2.5	What if students want additional lessons or classes beyond those detailed in the agreement?
2.6	Equipment and materials required/provided
2.7	The expiry date for all remaining unused lessons

2.8	Payment conditions (e.g., hourly rates, per week, per course, or seminar-workshop)
2.9	Travel costs (e.g., bus, train, parking) and car kilometre or mileage allowance. Is travelling time included?
2.10	Cancellation policies for when students (or the teacher) are absent (e.g., sickness, holidays).

3.	**ONLINE COURSES** (see pages 59 and 62)
3.1	Contact information including postal address
3.2	The place and times of lessons
3.3	How often do the lessons take place? How many have been agreed and booked?
3.4	What if students want additional lessons or classes beyond those detailed in the agreement?
3.5	Date of trial testing for equipment and broadband connection?

3.6	Equipment, materials, and VoIP[2] programs required
3.7	The start and finish dates
3.8	The expiry date for all remaining unused lessons
3.9	Regulations for lateness (see page 60)
3.10	Regulations for connection problems (see page 60)
3.11	Payment conditions (e.g., hourly rates, per week, per course, or seminar-workshop)
3.12	Expected behaviour and appearance during online sessions
3.13	Flaming and misbehaviour (see page 59)
3.14	Cancellation policies for when students (or the teacher) are absent (e.g., sickness, holidays)

---

[2] Voice Over Internet Protocol (VoIP) technological programs such as *Zoom, MS Teams, Google Hangouts, Skype,* and Teacher/Student software platforms.

What additional information needs to be included?

4.	Health and learning issues (see page 59)
4.1	Are there any health and medical conditions which may affect the (online) interaction and learning experience?
4.2	Are there any learning issues that may affect the (online) interaction and learning experience? (see page 59)

5.	Expected performance or objectives of the enrolling student or company
5.1	Does the company (or private student) expect the contract to itemise and cover expected performance and achievement goals? If so, what are they?

6.	**Intellectual property (IP), assignment, copyright**
	Who owns the IP, assignment and copyright ownership of materials produced?
6.1	Who owns the copyright of materials created and produced (during your tuition/training)?
	NOTE: *Many educational institutions keep copyright ownership of all materials produced and created by freelance teachers. You cannot use these materials to leverage passive income products.*
6.2	Photocopies?

7.	**General Data Protection Regulation Clause**
	(see page 65)
	The European Union General Data Protection Regulation (EU GDPR) imposes obligations onto organisations anywhere in the world as long as they target or collect data related to people in the EU.
7.1	Inserted?

To be included between you and your direct and/or associate customers

8.	**PRICES AND PAYMENT POLICIES**
	Are the pricing levels different between direct customers (private students and companies) and associate customers (language schools or other educational institutions)?
8.1	Do you require different contracts for different customers?
8.2	What are the payment terms for direct customers?
8.3	What are the payment terms for private students?
8.4	What are the payment terms for associate customers?
8.5	Preparation time?
8.6	Time to mark work?
8.7	Travel costs?
8.8	Is time spent between consecutive tuition slots within the same company included or excluded (e.g., coffee and lunch breaks) from your chargeable fee?

9.	Late payment policies
	*If payments are delayed, wave your contract before the student or company, and show them what was agreed. Of course, the most straightforward and most effective solution is to have direct customers **pay in advance**.*
9.1	Pay in advance?
9.2	Alternative ideas?
9.3	Refund policies?

10.	Insurances and limitation of liabilities (see page 57)
10.1	Do you and/or the student or company need a clause covering injury and death?
10.2	Do you and/or the student or company need a clause covering damage to equipment or the property (location of lessons or seminar-workshops)?

11.	**Cancellation policies**
11.1	Is there a cooling-off period?
11.2	Reasons and causes for immediate agreement termination

12.	**Holiday periods, sickness and absenteeism (short and prolonged)**
12.1	What is the procedure for cancelling a session because of illness or unforeseen situations?
12.2	Can lessons or seminar-workshops be postponed should the customer (or the teacher) become ill?
12.3	What is the procedure for when the student is sick or absent for long periods?
12.4	What is the procedure for when you (the teacher) is sick or absent for long periods?
12.5	What are the consequences (either the student or the teacher) when they are absent without prior notice?

13.	**WORKING CONDITIONS**
	What working conditions are different? Where do you give your tuition? For example, do you teach in your own classroom/home or at the student's, company's or school's premises?
13.1	Coffee and lunch breaks? When yes, who provides or pays for catering?
13.2	Travel costs? Hotel costs?
13.3	Limitation of liabilities and insurance coverage? (*Damages and injuries;* see page 57)
13.4	Is an *Independent Contractor Relationship* clause required for legal reasons in your country? (see page 54)

14.	**What do you expect private students, companies, schools, or institutions to provide?**
	This question depends on the freelancer's teaching field.
14.1	Classroom, office, conference room, seminar-workshop room, auditorium

14.2	Availability of schooling material and expendable supplies? Whiteboards and pens. Flipchart and markers. Blackboards, chalk and board cleaners. Foils for overhead projectors. Replacement flipchart paper, etc.
14.3	Electrical equipment? Computer and IT (internet technology) facilities? TV, overhead projector, audio equipment, etc.
14.4	When equipment (e.g., computer) doesn't work, and bulbs need replacing, who is responsible for providing assistance when Murphy's Law strikes?

15.	Clauses to be checked by a lawyer
	Where contracts are more complicated and depend on the situation and risk involved (e.g., a high penalty for non-delivery), it is advisable to ask a lawyer for assistance.
15.1	Do you require a lawyer to double-check clauses that have been requested or rewritten by customers?

Contract Blueprint

---

§§ § § § §§

A lawyer gives the stamp of approval to your teaching service contract

You want to prepare a contract as a foundation for your work. It must establish shared communications between yourself and the customer and detail the receiving and giving tuition. It also sets the groundwork for negotiations when things go wrong.

Hiring a lawyer to write a contract is the easiest strategy but also the most expensive in terms of money and time. And unfortunately, not feasible for many. Nonetheless, a self-made teaching service contract is still better than none.

Freelance teachers who decide to work alone after years of working for companies, schools and institutions, find it a major mental leap to offer their services directly to private students and companies.

They've invested a lot of time and energy into teaching methodologies and materials, but now they are confronted with other business aspects that associate customers normally take care of.

A teaching service contract is one of them—an important one.

However, if you have never prepared a business contract before, creating one from scratch may be quite daunting. My experience shows it helps when an example can be used as a first outline—a structural framework—that can be adjusted and changed to fit the provided teaching service.

The following contract example is a self-made agreement written during my time in Germany that I have overworked and extended for this book.

Read the example and additional clause examples. Then, pick-and-choose and change those parts that best fit your teaching niche purposes.

I suggest preparing templates for *all* your customers:

- Direct customers (students for private tuition)
- Direct customers (companies)
- Associate customers (schools and institutes)

Disclaimer

The following Teaching Service Contract *and* the Data Protection Agreement (Privacy Policy) for websites are exemplary samples for educational demonstration purposes only.

NEITHER the contract nor the Privacy Policy for websites have been approved by a lawyer.

Please remember that each country has its own tax rules and regulations. When unsure, consult a lawyer versed in company and taxation rules of the country where you are working and running your teaching business.

And please also be aware that not all countries outside the European Union are bound by the EU Data Protection Agreement.

The example teaching service contract on the following pages has been developed over the years I've worked as an English freelance language teacher in Germany. It's not exhaustive, and I cannot be held responsible for any misunderstandings or issues resulting from my example. To reiterate: **The example contract has NOT been controlled by a lawyer.**

The Data Protection Agreement rules and Independent Contractor Relationship Clause are the result of my researches on the Internet and are NOT necessarily correctly portrayed. Again, the purpose of the examples in this book is solely for educational demonstration.

It is recommended to obtain proper legal advice from the country you work in if you want a correctly formulated service contract and data protection agreement written by a lawyer.

EXAMPLE of a Teaching Service Contract

(for educational demonstration only)

between

Name: *« Trainer's name/Teaching service name »*

Address: *« Trainer's (or teaching service) address »*

Telephone: « ... »

Mobile: « ... »

E-mail: « ... »

and

Name: *« Student's name »*

Address *« Student's company name » and « address »*

Telephone: « ... »

Mobile: « ... »

E-mail: « ... »

For students who are minor (underaged)

- Parent/Guardian/Carer: *« Name »*

- Providing [online] lessons for: *« Minor(s) name(s) »*

- If the *« Minor name »* is under *« Legal minor age »*, the *parent/guardian/carer* gives permission for the *« Trainer's name »* to teach *« Minor name »*.

COURSE NAME / DESCRIPTION   « ... »

Private lessons for   *« Student(s) name(s) »*
Trainer: *« Trainer's name »*

AGREED TERMS

1   Lessons take place: *« how many times a week/month? »*

2   First course day: *« date », « time »*

3   Location/Office: *« place », « classroom/office »*

Location thoughts

- **Online:** computer, tablet, mobile telephone via VoIP technology

  Voice Over Internet Protocol (VoIP) technological programs such as *Zoom, MS Teams, Google Hangouts, Skype*, Teacher/Student software platforms.

  « Student » is required to connect to their *« lesson/class »* from a quiet environment such as their own home or conference room in which the lesson will not be disturbed.

- Face-to-face (address)

  School classroom, conference room, at home

---

4   EXPECTED OBJECTIVES (ACHIEVEMENT GOALS)

4.1   *« Describe the customer's aim, goal and skill expectation from your course. »*

4.2 The teaching material is compiled by the trainer based on placement tests and/or placement interviews and on agreed objectives (see 4.1 above). Exception: any textbook(s) requested by the *« Student/Company »*.

4.3 *« Lessons/classes »* are non-transferable.

5 PROVISION OF FACILITIES: *« Student/Company »*

5.1 *« Electrical equipment? Computer and IT (internet technology) facilities? »*

Equipment thoughts

- **Online:** computer, tablet, mobile telephone via VoIP technology

- Face-to-face tuition/seminar-workshops

  For example: Course books, handouts, whiteboards, flip charts, computer/overhead projector, audio equipment

---

6 INTELLECTUAL PROPERTY (IP), ASSIGNMENT, COPYRIGHT

6.1 The Intellectual Property (IP), assignment and copyright ownership of all educational materials created and recorded lessons produced for *« Student/Company »* during *« Course name /description »* are retained solely by *« Trainer's name »*.

6.2 Teaching materials may be used for educational, non-commercial purposes only. All materials used must be accredited to *« Trainer's name »*. *« Student/Company »* wishing to use such material for any other purpose should contact *« Trainer's name »*.

6.3 *« Student/Company »* undertake not to make unlawful photocopies.

7 TUITION FEES AND DURATION ARE

7.1 Fees are subject to annual review. Where prices are increased as a result of such a review, *« Trainer's name »* shall endeavour to give the *« Student/Company »* at least one month's notice of such increase.

7.2 Fees are: ☐ inc. VAT ☐ ex. VAT (*Value Added Tax*)

7.3 One standard lesson = 45 minutes at *« € ... »*

7.4 One double lesson = 90 minutes at *« € ... »*

7.5 Block bookings at *« € ... »*

8 VALIDITY AND EXPIRATION DATE OF LESSONS/CLASSES

8.1 Block bookings and booked standard and double lessons must be used up within one year. If these are not used within this period, they are expired.

8.2 The one-year period begins with the first lesson.

9 PAYMENT

9.1 The sale of « *Trainer's name/Teaching service* » services will not be considered definitive until after a quotation has been drawn up by « *Trainer's name* » and the acknowledgement of the order confirmation has been sent to the « *Trainer's name* » « *Student/Company* » by e-mail.

9.2 The quotations drawn up by « *Trainer's name* » are valid for a duration of « *number* » days.

9.3 Payment shall be made by bank transfer (without cash) immediately after receipt of the invoice and without discount to the following bank account: « *...* »

9.4 « *Seminar-workshops* », individual « *lessons/classes* », as well as block bookings are bound to the contracting party.

10 BILLING CONDITIONS

10.1 Payment for the « *lessons/classes* » is due in full by bank transfer before they begin.

10.2 Standard lessons and double lessons are payable in full in advance.

10.3 Block bookings are payable in full in advance or in monthly instalments when agreed with « *Trainer's name* ».

10.4 The number of monthly lessons is to be agreed upon in advance.

☐ Monthly payment: according to the number of lessons to be given (per lesson = « € ... »)
☐ Full payment: « € ... »

10.5 The balance of unused block bookings will be invoiced as payable in the twelfth month and paid accordingly.

10.6 Travel costs will be charged at « € ... » per « *kilometre/miles* » when the distance is more than « *... kilometre/miles* » between the « *Trainer's name* » address and the « *Student's/Company's* » address.

(Double-check your country tax requirements.)

10.7 VAT (Value Added Tax) « *is/is not* » applicable for « *add the appropriate tax clause of your country for freelance service providers* ».

(Double-check the tax requirements of your country.)

11   LATE PAYMENT PENALTIES

11.1 Late payment and breach of payment is subject to late payment interest. The late penalty charge amount results from applying the legal interest rate in force to the amounts still due at the time of the incident.

11.2 Any amount not paid when due will bear interest from the due date until paid at a rate equal to « ...% » per month (« ...% » annually) or the maximum allowed by law, whichever is less.

11.3 Fixed compensation for collection costs due to « *Trainer's name/Teaching service* » in the event of late payment: « € ... ».

12   REFUNDS

12.1 No refunds are given for pre-paid tuition under any circumstances.

12.2 « *Lessons/Classes* » are non-transferable.

13   HOLIDAY PERIODS, SICKNESS AND ABSENTEEISM POLICY

13.1 Statutory and Public holidays: « *lessons/classes* » are automatically cancelled.

☐ « *Lesson/Class* » fees are waived.

☐ « *Lesson/Class* » fees are continued during statutory and public holidays.

13.2 If the « *Student/Company* » has to cancel lessons, « *Trainer's name* » must be notified at least « *number* » working days in advance (by e-mail, SMS/Text or phone call). After which, a suitable replacement date must be arranged.

13.3 *« Number »* weeks of notice must be given for extended periods of absence.

13.4 Missed *« lessons/classes »* will be charged in full when the cancellation time limit is not honoured.

13.5 If *« Student's name »* becomes ill, the number of absent *« lessons/classes »* will be recovered in agreement with *« Trainer's name ».* In such cases, a medical certificate is required by *« Trainer's name and/or teaching service name ».*

13.6 If *« Trainer's name »* has to cancel *« lessons/classes »*, the *« Student/Company* will be informed at least 24 hours in advance. The number of absent *« lessons/classes »* will be recovered in agreement with the *« Student/Company »* to another date.

13.7 If *« Trainer's name »* becomes ill, the number of absent *« lessons/classes »* will be recovered in agreement with the *« Student/Company ».*

14 CANCELLATION POLICY

14.1 Neither *« Trainer's name and/or teaching service name »* and *« Student/Company »* shall be liable for any breach by the other party of any terms and conditions occasioned by pandemic (including the current Covid-19), any act of God, war, civil disturbance, strike, lock-out, flood, fire or other cause that cannot be avoided within the party's reasonable control.

14.2 A decision to discontinue « *lessons/classes* » requires « *number of days/weeks* » written notice (e-mail or letter) and shall be given by the party seeking to discontinue. If the « *Student/Company* » terminates « *lessons/classes* » with insufficient notice, the « *Student/Company* » will be liable to pay fees for those « *lessons/classes* » not taken during the notice period.

14.3 A decision to discontinue is excluded when the first « *lesson/class* » has already taken place with pre-paid block bookings.

14.4 A decision to discontinue is excluded for pre-paid individual lessons when the « *Trainer's name* » has not been notified at least « *number* » working days in advance.

14.5 « *Trainer's name* » reserves the right to dissolve the contractual relationship with immediate effect in the event of non-compliance with this agreement, in particular with regard to absenteeism and non-payment.

15 COMPLAINTS/GRIEVANCES

15.1 Should disputes arise during the term of this agreement, it is expected that discussions take place between the « *Trainer's name and/or teaching service name* » and « *Student/Company* » to resolve any dispute.

15.2 Any complaints or disputes should be addressed to « *Trainer's name* » in writing (e-mail or letter) and settled outside of « *lessons/classes* ». However, if the « *Trainer's name and/or teaching service name* » and « *Student/Company* » cannot resolve the complaint or dispute, they may agree to terminate this agreement with immediate effect or seek the services of a mediator.

16   GOVERNING LAW (DISPUTES AND COURT SETTLEMENTS)

16.1 This agreement shall be governed by « *Trainer's country of residence* » law in every particular.

16.2 **Jurisdiction for all claims** arising from this agreement is the nearest local court to « *Trainer's address* ».

17   GENERAL DATA PROTECTION REGULATION

17.1 The « *Trainer's name* » and « *Student/Company* » agrees to comply with all applicable laws, statutes, regulations, including in relation to confidentiality, privacy, GDPR[3] and the protection of personal data.

---

[3] Clause is **obligatory**: The European Union General Data Protection Regulation (**EU GDPR**) is a law that regulates the collection and processing of personal data within the EU and European Economic Area (EEA). The law requires a clause confirming that both parties know of and abide by this law.

18 SEVERABILITY CLAUSE

18.1 Should the foregoing agreement be wholly or in partial or invalid or inoperative or ineffective, the remaining provisions shall remain in state and in effect. Any paragraph or clause deemed invalid, inoperative, ineffective or becomes legally unworkable within the agreement is to be replaced by one that meets the agreement's purpose as closely as possible.

(SIGNATURE)

« Student/Company representative »
(Place + date)

(SIGNATURE)

« Trainer's name »
(Place + date)

Miscellaneous Optional Additions—Examples

(for educational demonstration purposes only)

Independent Contractor Relationship Clause

The following clause example can be added when teaching freelancers wish to avoid the consequences of:

- *An unwanted legal relationship where it may create undesired (financial or tax) obligations*

For example, the trainer is not entering an employer-employee relationship but is a self-employed individual who pays self-employment taxes.

- *Freelancers are contracted to do the work for a company according to the company's own processes and methods.*

For example, when teaching [language] freelancers want to avoid situations where their contractor (the company) tries to insist that they attend meetings outside classes or perform large translation jobs above and beyond what is specifically written and mutually agreed upon in the teaching service contract.

Example: INDEPENDENT CONTRACTOR RELATIONSHIP CLAUSE

- It is expressly agreed that the « *Trainer's name and/or teaching service name* » and the « *Company's name* » shall be independent contractors and that the relationship between the « *Trainer's name and/or teaching service name* » and the « *Company's name* » shall not constitute a partnership, joint venture, or agency. Neither « *Trainer's name and/or teaching service name* » and the « *Company's name* » shall have the power or right to bind or obligate the other party, nor represent that it has such authority.

Non-Compete/Non-Soliciting Agreement

A standard non-compete agreement restricts freelancers' activities when they leave their current associate customers (e.g., educational institutes). Such clauses state that the freelancer cannot engage in any employment activities that compete or conflict with the educational institute, school, or company for a certain number of years. Customers often want to keep their instructor for several reasons. There can be manifold reasons, but none are worthwhile violating any anti-competition clauses. Freelancers can incur heavy fines when caught stealing students—'poaching' as it is called—from a subcontractor or an associate's list of customers.

Example: NON-COMPETE/NON-SOLICITING CLAUSE

- After termination of this agreement for a period of « *number* » year(s) following the termination of « *Trainer's name* » employment and « *Trainer's name* » relationship with the « *Institute's name* », « *Trainer's name* » shall not, directly or indirectly, disclose to any person, company or corporation the names or addresses of any customers or clients of the « *Institute's name* » or any other information pertaining to them. Neither shall « *Trainer's name* » call on, solicit, take away, or attempt to visit and persuade any customer of the « *Institute's name* » that « *Trainer's name* » has come into contact with, or has become acquainted with, or has worked with during the term of « *Trainer's name* » employment as the direct or indirect result of « *Trainer's name* » employment with the « *Institute's name* ».

Examples: COOLING-OFF PERIOD

- The agreement cooling-off period starts from the date of the contract and ends « *number of days* » later.

- If the « *Student/Company* » decide to change their mind and no longer wish to receive « *lessons/classes* » from « *Trainer's name* », « *Student/Company* » has a right to cancel the « *lessons/classes* » within a cooling-off period of « *number of days* ».

- To cancel the contract, the « *Student/Company* » must inform « *Trainer's name* » of the decision to cancel the contract during the cooling-off period in writing by e-mail, letter, or SMS/Text.

- The « *Student/Company* » will receive a refund for « *lessons/classes* » paid but not received within the cooling-off period prior to cancellation.

Example: LEARNING GUARANTEE

- « *Trainer's name* » will ensure « *lessons/classes* » are prepared and carried out to the best of « *his/her* » ability to safeguard « *Student's/Company's* » satisfactory progress. Learning success of « *Student/Company* » cannot be guaranteed. A prerequisite for successful learning is a methodical and consistent practice as advised by « *Trainer's name* ».

Example: ADDITIONAL LESSONS

- Additional « *lessons/classes* » may be scheduled during holiday periods, by mutual agreement and at a fee mutually agreed between the « *Student/Company* » and « *Trainer's name* ».

Example: TRANSLATION WORK

- « *Trainer's name* » will help with letters or short translations but is not obliged to do complete translations. For such tasks, « *Trainer's name* » translation service is at your disposal.

Examples: INSURANCE/LIABILITIES

DAMAGES AND INJURIES

- The « *Student/Company* » is responsible for ensuring insurance coverage in the case of death or personal injury during « *lessons/classes* » that is not foreseeable or has occurred due to negligence.

- The « *Trainer's name* » is not liable for death or personal injury during « *lessons/classes* » caused by negligence, fraud, or fraudulent misrepresentation.

SPACE AND EQUIPMENT

- The « *Student/Company* » is responsible for ensuring insurance coverage in the case of any loss or damage to any equipment, inventory, or to the property used in connection with the provision of « *lessons/classes* » that is not foreseeable or has occurred as a result of negligence.

- « *Trainer's name* » is not liable for any technical faults, failures or damages of equipment used at the « *Student's/Company's* » premises or elsewhere for providing tuition. « *Trainer's name* » will not be required to make up for any lost teaching time caused by such technical faults, failures or damages. Moving equipment to enhance the quality of TV/video/audio is done at the « *Student's/Company's* » risk.

Additional Clause Ideas for ONLINE Courses

Examples: HEALTH AND LEARNING ISSUES

- The « *Student/company/parent/guardian/carer* » is responsible for informing « *Trainer's name* » of any health and medical conditions which may affect the online interaction and learning experience.

- The « *Student/company/parent/guardian/carer* » is responsible for informing « *Trainer's name* » of any learning disabilities which may affect the online interaction and learning experience.

Examples: FLAMING AND MISBEHAVIOUR

- Any defamatory, offensive or illegal material published online by « *Student's name* » or inappropriate behaviour by « *Student's name* » will immediately end the « *lessons/classes* » and constitutes a breach of the agreement.

- What constitutes such behaviour will be determined in the reasonable opinion of « *Trainer's name* ». In this instance, « *Trainer's name* » reserves the right to terminate this agreement with immediate effect. Fees paid will not be refunded.

Examples: LATENESS

- The « *Student/Company* » must be on time for « *lessons/classes* » and must log in to video chat five minutes before the « *lesson/class* » is due to start.
- The « *Student/Company* » must inform « *Trainer's name* » of a late arrival to class 60 minutes before the lesson start time (by e-mail, SMS/Text or phone call).
- If the « *Student/Company* » is more than ten minutes late for a lesson and has not informed « *Trainer's name* » prior to the lesson, « *Trainer's name* » reserves the right to cancel without refund or rescheduling.
- If the « *Student/Company* » is late and has informed « *Trainer's name* » before the class, the lost time is either added to a future « *lesson/class* » or the « *lesson/class* » is rescheduled.

Examples: CONNECTION PROBLEMS

- The « *lesson/class* » trial lesson serves to check that the Internet connection used by the « *Student/Company* » is of sufficient quality to undertake online lessons. No refunds are given due to connection quality or speed.

- The « *Student/Company* » must possess the following:

  o A broadband internet connection.
  o The latest version of « *required VoIP technical programs* such as Zoom, MS Teams, Google Hangouts, Skype, Teacher/Student software platforms. »
  o A microphone headset or a pair of headphones
  o A webcam

- The « *Student/Company* » must log in to « *required VoIP technical program* » at least 5 minutes before the lesson starts to ensure the Internet connection and audio equipment are functioning correctly.

- If « *Trainer's name* » has a technical problem that lasts less than 15 minutes during the lesson, the lost time will be caught up in the following « *lesson/class* ». If the problem lasts more than 15 minutes, « *Trainer's name* » will reschedule the « *lesson/class* ».

- If the « *Student/Company* » has a technical problem, the lesson can be neither refunded nor rescheduled.

- « *Trainer's name* » is not required to make up lost time due to technical difficulties experienced at the « *Student's/Company's* » home or other location used for providing online tuition (e.g., insufficient or unreliable audio and video broadband, poor sound quality, computer hardware and software problems).

Examples: ONLINE MINOR STUDENTS

Space and equipment

- The *« School/parent/guardian/carer »* is responsible for providing suitable space and appropriate technology to enable online learning to be delivered as advised by *« Trainer's name »*.

- The *« School/parent/guardian/carer »* is responsible for ensuring that the online teaching platform recommended by *« Trainer's name »* is installed and ready for use prior to the beginning of *« lessons/classes »*. All technical issues should be referred to the software/platform provider.

- The *« Parent/guardian/carer »* is responsible for ensuring that the *« Minor »* is available for the arranged online *« lessons/classes »* as confirmed by e-mail between *« Trainer's name »* and *« Parent/guardian/carer »*. Any delays or interruptions encroaching into the *« lesson/class »* time is considered as time provided.

- Both *« Trainer's name »* and *« Minor's name »* must dress appropriately for the online lesson.

- Both *« Trainer's name »* and *« Minor's name »* should present against a neat and tidy background when using video.

- The *« Parent/guardian/carer »* may, if they wish, be present during the online lesson if *« Trainer's name »* agrees and gives permission.

- Materials supplied electronically by *« Trainer's name »* remain the Intellectual Property of *« Trainer's name ».* *« School/parent/guardian/carer »* undertake not to make unlawful photocopies.

- *« Trainer's name »* is not liable for any technical faults, failures or damages of equipment used at the *« Minor/school/parent/guardian/carer's »* premises or elsewhere for providing online tuition.

- Moving any equipment to enhance the quality of TV/video/audio is done at the *« Minor/school/parent /guardian/carer's »* risk. *« Trainer's name »* will not be required to make up for any lost teaching time caused by faults, failures or damages as a result of moving equipment.

- *« Trainer's name »* is not required to make up lost time due to technical difficulties experienced at the *« Minor/school/parent/guardian/carer's »* home or other location used for providing online teaching (e.g., insufficient or unreliable audio and video broadband, poor sound quality, computer hardware and software problems).

- The decision to discontinue lessons by the « *Parent/guardian/carer* » or « *Trainer's name* » requires « *number of days/weeks* » written notice (e-mail or letter).

- If the « *Parent/guardian/carer* » discontinues lessons with insufficient notice, the « *Parent/guardian/carer* » will be liable to pay fees for « *lessons/classes* » not taken during the notice period.

- If no notice to discontinue « *lessons/classes* » has been served and the « *Minor* » misses an arranged online « *lesson/class* » as confirmed by e-mail between « *Trainer's name* » and « *Parent/guardian/carer* », fees for that « *lesson/class* » remain payable and no refund of any fees paid in advance will be given.

Websites and Data Protection Agreement (GDPR)

---

*The **General Data Protection Regulation (GDPR)** is the toughest privacy and security law in the world. Though it was drafted and passed by the European Union (EU), it imposes obligations onto organisations anywhere, so long as they target or collect data related to people in the EU.*

What is GDPR, the EU's new data protection law?—GDPR.eu. ***https://gdpr.eu/what-is-gdpr/*** *and* ***https://gdpr.eu/checklist/***

The EU General Data Protection law

The EU GDPR (European Union General Data Protection Regulation) of 25 May 2018 regulates the collection and processing of personal data within the EU and European Economic Area (EEA). It imposes obligations onto organisations anywhere in the world as long as they target or collect data related to people in the EU. More information can be found on the **European Commission** website:

- *https://ec.europa.eu/info/index_en*
- *https://ec.europa.eu/info/law/law-topic/data-protection_en*

The **EEAS (European External Action Service) homepage:** See below their website example (*Table of Contents EEAS—About Us*) of a privacy statement concerning the processing and the protection of personal data given by the **Publications Office of the European Union:**

• *https://op.europa.eu/en/web/about-us/legal-notices/op_whoiswho*

Table of Contents—EEAS About Us

1. Introduction

2. Why and how do we process your personal data?

3. On what legal ground(s) do we process your personal data?

4. Which personal data do we collect and further process?

5. How long do we keep your personal data?

6. How do we protect and safeguard your personal data?

7. Who has access to your personal data, and to whom is it disclosed?

8. What are your rights, and how can you exercise them?

9. Contact information

10. Where to find more detailed information?

The regulation requires freelancers to attach an additional Data Protection Agreement clause to their contract and define them in their website Privacy Policy and Terms & Conditions.

Yes, it does go beyond the focus of writing teaching contracts. Still, I believe freelance teaching colleagues with websites will appreciate having an example to help them meet with the **EU GDPR** law.

Data Protection Agreement for Websites

(EXAMPLE for educational demonstration)

1   YOUR LEGAL RIGHTS

According to EU legislation, « *Students/Companies* » based in the European Union have a permanent right to access, modify, rectify and rebut their personal information. This right can be exercised by contacting « *Trainer's name* » by e-mail.

2   DATA RETENTION

What data does « *Trainer's name and/or teaching service name* » collect about « *Student/Company* », for what purpose and on what ground does « *Trainer's name and/or teaching service name* » process it.

Personal data means any information capable of identifying an individual. It does not include anonymised data. « *Trainer's name and/or teaching service name* » may process the following categories of personal data about « *Student/Company* »:

2.1 Communication Data

Communication data includes any communication that « *Student/Company* » sends through e-mail, social media messaging, social media posting, or any other communication. « *Trainer's name and/or teaching service name* » process this data to communicate with « *Student/Company* » for record-keeping and for the establishment, pursuance, or defence of legal claims. « *Trainer's name and/or teaching service name* » lawful ground for this processing is their legitimate interests which in this case are to reply to communications sent to them, to keep records and to establish, pursue or defend legal claims.

2.2 Customer Data

Customer data includes data relating to any purchases of goods and/or services from « *Trainer's name and/or teaching service name* », such as « *Student's/Company's* »name, title, invoicing address, delivery address, e-mail address, telephone number, contact details, purchase details, and « *Student's/Company's* »card details. « *Trainer's name and/or teaching service name* » process this data to supply the goods and/or services « *Student/Company* » have purchased and to keep records of such transactions. *« Trainer's name and/or teaching service name »* lawful ground for this processing is the performance of a contract between *« Student/Company »* and *« Trainer's name and/or teaching service name »* and/or taking steps at *« Student/Company »* request to enter into such a contract.

2.3 User Data

User data that includes data about how *« Student/Company »* use *« Trainer's name and/or teaching service name »* website and any online services together with any data that *« Student/Company »* post for publication on their website or through other online services.

« Trainer's name and/or teaching service name » lawful ground for this processing is their legitimate interests which in this case are to enable them to administer their website and their business correctly.

2.4 Technical Data

Technical data that includes data about *« Student's/Company's »* use of *« Trainer's name and/or teaching service name »* website and online services such as *« Student's/Company's »* IP address, login data, details about their browser, length of visit to pages on *« Trainer's name and/or teaching service name »* website, page views and navigation paths, details about the number of times *« Student/Company »* use *« Trainer's name and/or teaching service name »* website, time zone settings and other technology on the devices *« Student/Company »* use to access *« Trainer's name and/or teaching service name »* website. The source of this data is the *« Trainer's name and/or teaching service name »* analytics tracking system.

« Trainer's name and/or teaching service name » process this data to analyse *« Student's/Company's »* use of *« Trainer's name and/or teaching service name »* website and online services, to administer and protect their business and website, and to provide relevant content to *« Student/Company »*.

« Trainer's name and/or teaching service name » lawful ground for this processing is their legitimate interests to enable them to administer their website and their business properly and to grow *« Trainer's name and/or teaching service name »* business and to decide their marketing strategy.

2.5 Marketing Data

Marketing Data that includes data about *« Student's/Company's »* preferences in receiving marketing from *« Trainer's name and/or teaching service name »* and *« Student's/Company's »* communication preferences.

« *Trainer's* name » may use Customer Data, User Data, Technical Data and Marketing Data to deliver relevant website content to « *Student/Company* » and to measure or understand the effectiveness of the content « *Trainer's name and/or teaching service name* » provide « *Student/Company* ». Their lawful ground for this processing is legitimate interests to grow their business. « *Trainer's name and/or teaching service name* » may also use such data to send other marketing communications to « *Student/Company* ». Their lawful ground for this processing is either consent or legitimate interests to grow their business.

2.6 Sensitive Data

« *Trainer's name and/or teaching service name* » do not collect any Sensitive Data about « *Student/Company* ». Sensitive data refers to data that includes details about « *Student's/Company's* » race or ethnicity, religious or philosophical beliefs, sex life, sexual orientation, political opinions, trade union membership, information about their health and genetic and biometric data. « *Trainer's name and/or teaching service name* » do not collect any information about criminal convictions and offences.

Where « *Trainer's name and/or teaching service name* » are required to collect personal data by law under the terms of the contract between « *Trainer's name and/or teaching service name* », and where « *Student/Company* » does not provide that data when requested, « *Trainer's name* » may not be able to fulfil the contract (e.g., to deliver goods or services to « *Student/Company* »). If « *Student/Company* » does not provide the requested data, « *Trainer's name and/or teaching service name* » may have to cancel a product or service ordered by « *Student/Company* ». If « *Trainer's name* » has to cancel a product or service requested by « *Student/Company* », « *Trainer's name and/or teaching service name* » will notify « *Student/Company* » at the time.

3   DISCLOSURES OF YOUR PERSONAL DATA

« *Trainer's name and/or teaching service name* » may have to share « *Student's/Company's* » personal data with the services and parties set out below:

- Service providers: providing IT and system administration services
- Government bodies requiring reported processing activities from « *Trainer's name and/or teaching service name* »
- Payment processors: managing online payments
- Online platforms hosting educational products (e.g., e-courses and e-books) and VoIP Teacher/Student teaching software platforms

- E-mail providers: marketing/list building services
- Website plugins: monitoring and protecting website security; spam prevention
- Google Analytics: website tracking purposes
- Embedded audio and video players
- Online scheduling services
- Website hosting services

« Trainer's name and/or teaching service name » require all third parties to whom *« Trainer's name and/or teaching service name »* transfer *« Student's/Company's »* data to respect the security of their personal data and to treat it in accordance with the law. *« Trainer's name and/or teaching service name »* only allow such third parties to process *« Student's/Company's »* personal data for specified purposes and in accordance with *« Trainer's name and/or teaching service name »* instructions.

4   DATA RETENTION

« Trainer's name » will only retain *« Student's/Company's »* personal data for as long as necessary to fulfil the purposes *« Trainer's name and/or teaching service name »* collected it for, including satisfying any legal, accounting, or reporting requirements.

When deciding what *« Student/Company »* data is the correct period to keep, *« Trainer's name and/or teaching service name* » will look at its amount, nature and sensitivity, potential risk of harm from unauthorised use or disclosure, the processing purposes, and if these can be achieved by other means and legal requirements.

The law requires « *Trainer's name and/or teaching service name* » to keep basic information about their customers for tax purposes (including Contact, Identity, Financial and Transaction Data), and which have to be kept for « *number* » years after « *Student/Company* » are no longer customers.

(SIGNATURE)   (SIGNATURE)

« Student/Company representative »   *« Trainer's name »*
(Place + date)   *(Place + date)*

Did You Find This Book Helpful?

Reviews are the heart and soul of a book's success. Only a good list of reviews encourages our colleagues to find it.

You can make an enormous difference. Because when you write a review, you'll be helping friends and colleagues discover useful books. And you will help authors—including myself—to keep writing them. Readers will often pass a book no matter how interesting it sounds or how great the cover is. Those stars and a few words have a huge impact.

This book will only be read if you tell readers about it. It would mean so much to me if you shared your view about it. It takes only a minute or two to leave an honest review at your preferred book retailer.

Your recommendation would help friends and colleagues decide which books they should spend their money and time.

Thank you in advance.

Janine

About the Author

Teaching English has been my business and passion—reading and painting my second passion.

I've been freelancing for around thirty years. Semi-retired, I am now writing a series of books giving practical marketing and business advice for teaching freelancers. I plan my books to help colleagues find students and earn enough to live from their profession.

I have worked in the Sales and Marketing departments in Belgium and Germany and completed a two-term voluntary member of the IATEFL[4] Executive Marketing Committee. Marketing was the key to helping me thrive in the freelance English language teaching market. As a result, I successfully avoided the **three-year death cycle most freelance teaching businesses[5] suffer.**

Meanwhile, I have been published in several language teaching magazines. Please get in touch if you have questions.

---

[4] IATEFL = International Association of Teachers of English as a Foreign Language

[5] Teaching businesses fail due to cash flow problems—they have insufficient cash to cover their current liabilities. Lack of money chokes many teaching services within a three-year cycle and is one condition that leads to the premature death of a teaching service business. My first book, *The Teacher's Guide to Pricing Matters*, describes what you can do to prevent this happening.

HOW TO CONNECT WITH ME

Website

Entrepreneurial Freelance Teachers

@

www.ft-training.com

Author website

@

www.braymueller.com

Facebook

www.facebook.com/FTTraining

LinkedIn

www.linkedin.com/company/freelance-teachers---training/

OTHER BOOKS WRITTEN BY JANINE BRAY-MUELLER

https://braymueller.com/books/

The Teacher's Guide to Pricing Matters

Quality Teaching Has Its Price

What should I charge? Freelancers who rely on *'the going rates'* continuously undercharge their teaching fees. Now they can work out an acceptable pricing rate commensurate with their skills and experience.

The Ultimate Guide to Teaching Niches

Stand out in a crowded teaching market and find a steady stream of students

How do you attract a steady flow of new students on the global teaching market? What you don't need are theoretical discussions about niches and specialising. Instead, you need a practical, hands-on system that works.

Tell me... What Do You Teach?

Marketing your teaching business to attract new customers

The importance of being different. When you know how to teach but don't know what to write in your promotional materials, you can't tell your students what they gain by attending your courses. **They won't come!** Create a spotlight for your teaching business and attract the attention of new customers.